Profiles in Greek and Roman Mythology

APOLLO

Mitchell Lane
PUBLISHERS

P.O. Box 196
Hockessin, Delaware 19707
Visit us on the web: www.mitchelllane.com
Comments? email us: mitchelllane@mitchelllane.com

PROFILES IN GREEK AND ROMAN MYTHOLOGY

Titles in the Series

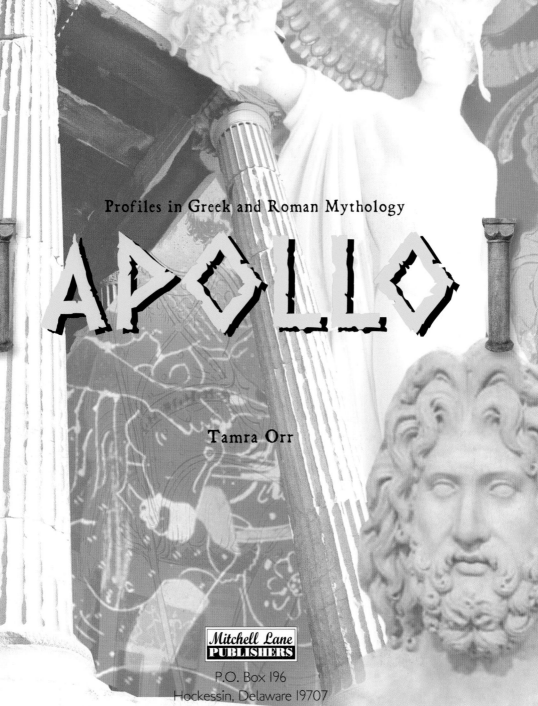

Profiles in Greek and Roman Mythology

APOLLO

Tamra Orr

Mitchell Lane
PUBLISHERS

P.O. Box 196
Hockessin, Delaware 19707
Visit us on the web: www.mitchelllane.com
Comments? email us: mitchelllane@mitchelllane.com

Printing   3   4   5   6   7   8   9

Library of Congress Cataloging-in-Publication Data
Orr, Tamra.
  Apollo / by Tamra Orr.
       p. cm. — (Profiles in Greek and Roman mythology)
  Includes bibliographical references and index.
  ISBN 978-1-58415-704-5 (library bound)
  1. Apollo (Greek deity)—Juvenile literature. I. Title.
  BL820.A7O77 2009
  398.20938'01—dc22
                                                      2008020909

ABOUT THE AUTHOR: Tamra Orr is the author of more than 100 books for children of all ages. She lives in the Pacific Northwest with her four kids and husband. She has written more than a dozen books for Mitchell Lane Publishers, including *Jordin Sparks, Meet Our New Student From China, A Kid's Guide to Perennial Gardens, Care for a Potbellied Pig, Care for a Pet Ferret*, and the five-volume Money Matters series.

PUBLISHER'S NOTE: This story is based on the author's extensive research, which she believes to be accurate. Documentation of such research is contained on page 46.

The internet sites referenced herein were active as of the publication date. Due to the fleeting nature of some web sites, we cannot guarantee they will all be active when you are reading this book.

To reflect current usage, we have chosen to use the secular era designations BCE ("before the common era") and CE ("of the common era") instead of the traditional designations BC ("before Christ") and AD (*anno Domini,* "in the year of the Lord").

Every effort has been made to locate all copyright holders of material used in this book. If any errors or omissions have occurred, corrections will be made in future editions of this book.

PHOTO CREDITS: p. 6—artist John William Waterhouse; p. 12—artist François Girardon and Thomas Regnaudin; p. 15—artist Diana Scultori Ghisi; p. 16—artist Anicet-Charles-Gabriel Lemonnier; p. 17—artist Johann Wilhelm Baur; p. 18—artist François Le Moyne/JupiterImages; p. 20—Barbara Marvis; p. 24—artist Hendrick van Balen; p. 25—artist Pietro di Cristoforo Vannucci; p. 26—artist Melchior Meier; p. 30 (right)—François-Joseph Bosio; p. 31—artist Evelyn De Morgan; p. 33—artist Giovanni Battista Tiepolo; p. 34—Forest Glen Seminary; p. 36—Geslin Collection; p. 39—artist Giovanni Battista Tiepolo; p. 41—Gutenberg.org.

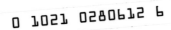

TABLE OF CONTENTS

Profiles in Greek and Roman Mythology

In *Apollo and Daphne,* created by John William Waterhouse in 1908, Apollo's fingers are just brushing the lovely Daphne as she turns into a tree. Although he was the god of light and music, Apollo had trouble with romance.

APOLLO

CHAPTER 1

Inspiration and Explanations

He glimpsed her again, gliding among the trees. The sun god Apollo (ah-PAH-loh) had seen the lovely Daphne (DAF-nee) running through the woods more times than he could count. The daughter of the river god Peneus (PEE-nee-us) loved running through the forest, playing by the babbling brooks, and talking to the birds. What she did not care for, however, was men. Her attitude did not dissuade Apollo. Struck by the arrows of Eros (AIR-os), the god of love and desire, Apollo thought Daphne was the most beautiful woman he had ever seen. He was determined to have her. When he found out that a young hero named Leucippus (LOO-kih-pus), son of King Oenomaus (ee-noh-MAY-us) of Pisa, also wanted Daphne, he arranged to bury the competition.

Leucippus was hiding among the other nymphs who spent their days frolicking with Daphne. Dressed like a girl, Leucippus mingled with the maidens, and no one suspected his presence. Scheming to ruin his happiness, Apollo convinced the nymphs to bathe in the nude. As they removed their clothing, they realized there was a traitor among them! The nymphs killed Leucippus. Apollo was delighted. With Leucippus gone, he could now get close to the beautiful Daphne.

As he ran after her, he tried to persuade Daphne to stop. "Stay, daughter of Peneus," he implored her. "I am not a foe. Do not fly from me as a lamb flies from the wolf, or a dove the hawk. It is for love I pursue you. . . . I am no clown, no rude peasant. Zeus [ZOOS] is my father!"[1] Surely she would be honored to be loved by a god, he reasoned.

Daphne ran on, calling to her father. "Help me, Peneus!" she exclaimed. "Open the earth to enclose me, or change my form, which has brought me into this danger!"[2]

Just as Apollo grasped her waist, her father turned her into a laurel tree. Apollo was left hugging nothing but a tree trunk. It was not the first or last time Apollo would lose someone he loved.

Apollo's Place in the Pantheon

The ancient Greeks believed in many gods, goddesses, demigods, nymphs, and other characters. The entire group of gods, called the pantheon, was headed by Zeus, their king. After Zeus, there were eleven major deities: Hera (HAYR-uh), wife of Zeus; Poseidon (poh-SY-dun), god of the sea; Hades (HAY-deez), god of the Underworld; Hestia (HES-tee-uh), goddess of the hearth, whose place would be taken by Dionysus (dy-uh-NY-sus), god of wine and ecstasy; Ares (AIR-eez), god of war; Athena (uh-THEE-nah), goddess of war and crafts; Artemis (AR-tuh-mis), goddess of the hunt; Aphrodite (aa-froh-DY-tee), goddess of love; Hermes (HUR-meez), messenger of the gods; and Hephaestus (heh-FES-tus), god of fire. Apollo was the twin brother of Artemis. He was the god of prophecy, music, and light, and he taught mortals about medicine. As god of light, he never told a lie. Associated with the sun god, Helios, his daily chore was to drive the sun across the sky in his chariot.

These twelve gods lived on Mount Olympus, and were called the Olympians. Other deities would join them, including Demeter (DIH-mih-ter), goddess of the harvest, and Hercules (HER-kyoo-leez), who guarded the gate. As the son of Zeus and Alcmene (alk-MEE-nee), a mortal woman, this hero was turned into a god at the end of his earthly life.

The Power of Myths

Tales of gods and goddesses have been passed down for more than three thousand years. For centuries, they were told out loud, as

Apollo (left) and Artemis were twins, but they had very different personalities. When they needed to, however, they could band together and wreak havoc upon others. They were a powerful pair.

songs, stories, and poems, by people with tremendous memories and dedication. These storytellers would wander from place to place, captivating people for hours with tales of jealousy, bravery, romance, or foolishness. Eventually the tales were written down, and what we know about the Greek deities and heroes and their adventures is largely based on these writings.

Homer's epics *The Iliad* and *The Odyssey* are two of the best-known sources for myths. It is believed that these two masterpieces had been recited for centuries by wandering poets, but Homer wrote them down and perfected them. As much information as they give us, however, these epics primarily center on the Trojan War and the aftermath only—a short era in the Greek and Roman period. Homer may have also written the *Homeric Hymns,* which were shorter poems that told of the adventures of the gods; however, some scholars date them from the sixth century BCE, decades after Homer's lifetime. Other written sources include *Theogony,* supposedly written by the poet Hesiod. It tells of the beginning of the world through the first marriage of Zeus. A composer named Pindar wrote musical tributes to some of the Greek winners of athletic games.

Other writers of Greek myths throughout the ages were the playwrights Aeschylus (ES-kuh-lis), Sophocles (SAH-fuh-kleez), and Euripides (yuh-RIP-ih-deez). Herodotus (her-AH-duh-tus) was known as the "father of history" for his accounts of the wars between the Greeks and Persians, while Callimachus (kuh-LIM-ah-kus) wrote poems about Zeus, Artemis, Athena, and other gods. The writings of Callimachus survived on hundreds of small pieces of papyrus, a paper-like material made from reeds. The wild adventures of Jason and the Argonauts come from Apollonius of Rhodes' epic *Argonautica*. Greek philosopher Plutarch wrote biographies of many famous Greeks and Romans, and Roman poet Virgil wrote the classic *Aeneid,* which tells how Rome was founded by a survivor of the Trojan War. Ovid's *Metamorphoses* is a fifteen-book poem and one of the best sources for myths. In it, Ovid relates the stories that involve shape-changing (metamorphoses), such as Daphne's transformation from a nymph to a laurel tree.

These stories were extremely important to the people of ancient Greece. For many, their main form of entertainment was listening to riveting stories of powerful deities and inspiring heroes. The stories also explained phenomena in their lives that they did not understand. Why did the sun rise? Where did it go at night? Why did the weather change? Why did some people get sick? How did the world begin, and what happened after a person died? Myths answered these questions. For the Greeks, the gods and goddesses directed life and death—and even the afterlife. The lives of mortals had meaning and purpose as long as the deities were doing their jobs. The gods were worshiped throughout ancient Greece in the home and in elaborate temples dedicated to them. Festivals were held in their honor.

Heroes also acted as inspiration to many. Their bravery in the face of monsters and massive armies was uplifting. Their mistakes proved that anyone could be a hero. Their romances—successful or otherwise—amused people. Their losses in war and in life echoed the losses people had to face every day, making hardships somehow more acceptable and easier to bear.

Apollo holds his lyre, the instrument he was best known for, on this vase.

Other than through ancient writings, the modern world knows about the lives of the heroes, gods, and goddesses in ancient myths through visual art. Important moments from some of the most popular stories were engraved on vases, painted on canvas, or sculpted in stone. They are on display in museums and art galleries all over the world, giving people a glimpse into the distant past.

The Greeks made vases in many shapes and sizes. The majority were made of clay, although some were made of metal. Usually, a special clay mixture was used to paint gods, goddesses, and heroes fighting battles, wooing lovers, clashing with monsters, or hunting unearthly creatures. Often the deities and heroes were shown holding the symbols that came to be associated with each of them. An oil flask, for example, shows Apollo holding a lyre; he is standing next to a palm tree to represent his place of birth.

When the vases were fired in the kiln, the clay mixture turned black, while the rest of the clay turned red-orange. Sometimes the artists would reverse the process. They would paint the background of the vase, which would turn black, and leave the designs in red-orange.

Another way that Greek figures were immortalized was through sculpture. Some sculptures were made as gifts to the gods or to be displayed in temples for worshiping. Made of clay, marble, or bronze, they were frequently painted in bright colors. In the Parthenon in Athens, a statue of Athena, made of gold and ivory, stood almost 40 feet (13 meters) tall. An equally tall statue of Zeus, also made of gold and ivory, and listed as one of the Seven Wonders of the Ancient World, was erected in the Temple of Zeus in Olympia. On the west pediment of Zeus' temple was a scene showing the battle between the centaurs and the Lapiths, with Apollo at the center.

Besides in Greece and Rome, museums around the world display pieces of ancient Greek and Roman art. The Metropolitan Museum in New York City, for example, has more than 35,000 pieces, from vases and statues to coins and jewelry.

This marble carving of *Apollo Tended by the Nymphs of Thetis,* by François Girardon and Thomas Regnaudin, was created for the gardens in Versailles, France. Apollo was always linked closely with the sea. The Greeks believed that the setting sun went underwater at the end of each day. As the sun god, Apollo supposedly went beneath the surface as well, where he was cared for by the nymphs of the sea goddess Thetis. The next morning, he would again ride his chariot across the sky, bringing sunlight back into the world.

APOLLO

CHAPTER 2
A Rough Beginning

From the moment he was born, Apollo was always chasing after something. It seemed to be part of his destiny. Sometimes he caught what he was after, and sometimes, as with Daphne, he just missed it.

Apollo's father was Zeus, king of all the Greek gods. Zeus could have almost any woman—mortal or not—that he wanted, and he often did. Most women could not resist a god as powerful as he. In addition to his wife, Hera, he had a number of girlfriends—much to Hera's dismay. One girlfriend, Leto (LEE-toh), the daughter to Coeus (KOY-us) and Phoebe (FEE-bee), became pregnant with Zeus' twins.

Hera was a jealous, powerful goddess with a wicked temper. When it came time for Leto to give birth, Hera decided to get revenge. First, she sent the dragon snake Python (PY-thon), offspring of Gaia (GY-uh), the mother earth, to chase Leto across the land. Hera declared that Leto would not be allowed to give birth on solid ground nor anywhere the sun shone. When Leto tried to escape across the water, some sources say that Hera sent the North Wind Boreas (BOHR-ee-us) to push her far out to sea. Others say that Zeus, in an attempt to protect Leto from jealous Hera, sent the wind to take Leto to his brother, Poseidon, god of the sea, for protection.

Finding a Birth Place

Leto traveled from one place to another, desperately pleading for someone to take her in. However, the people knew that if they did, Hera would punish them without mercy, so they refused her. They felt bad for Leto, but they were simply too afraid. Leto wandered throughout Crete and Athens and to many of the islands in the Aegean Sea. She was turned away at every stop.

Finally, she went to the floating island of Ortygia (or-TIH-jee-uh). Her sister Asteria lived there in the form of a quail. Earlier, Asteria had refused to become another one of Zeus' girlfriends, so he transformed her into a bird and cast her out to this island. Leto begged Asteria to be allowed onto Ortygia, promising that if her island would be her son's refuge, and the site of his temple, no one would try to take it over, and indeed people would bring riches to her land from far and wide. She also promised that Apollo would turn the island into a paradise and a haven for people who needed shelter and safety.[1] Asteria was tempted, but she was afraid that Apollo would not follow through on these promises. She made Leto swear on the River Styx, "the strongest and most awful oath for the blessed gods,"[2] that he would make his first temple there. Leto eagerly agreed.

Leto could finally give birth—but one element still stood in the way. Hera had declared she could not labor anywhere the sun shone. To help her, Poseidon raised the ocean's waves like a dome over the island. The sun could not get through. Soon, Leto gave birth to a girl, whom she named Artemis.

Hera was not finished interfering, however. Hoping to make Leto suffer longer, she purposely delayed Eileithyia (eyl-EYTH-ee-EYE-uh), goddess of childbirth, from going to Ortygia. The myth states that for nine days and nights, Leto did indeed suffer, because Artemis had a twin. Leto still had another baby to birth.

The goddesses with Leto finally gave Iris, a heavenly messenger, a gold and amber necklace as a bribe to bring Eileithyia to the island. Iris quietly snuck into Hera's palace and whispered to Eileithyia what was happening to Leto. The goddess took pity on the laboring mother and quickly turned into a dove, flying back to Ortygia before Hera noticed she was gone. According to the *Homeric Hymn to Apollo*, as soon as Eileithyia arrived, Leto threw her arms around a palm tree and at last gave birth to Apollo, "while the earth laughed for joy beneath. Then the child leaped forth to the light, and all the goddesses washed [him] purely and cleanly with sweet water, and

Latona Giving Birth to Apollo and Diana on the Island of Delos, an engraving from 1580 by Diana Scultori Ghisi. The Romans, who adopted many of the Greek myths, called Leto Latona and Artemis Diana. The artist's interpretation of Leto's childbirth shows the stress of endless days of hard labor, the manipulation of the gods, and the vengeance of Hera.

swathed [him] in a white garment of fine texture, new-woven, and fastened a golden band about [him]."[3]

Time for Revenge

At last, Leto's children had been born, despite Hera's plans to stop the birth. They were no ordinary babies. Bathed in ambrosia and nectar, in only a few days, both of them were fully grown. Apollo was a beautiful man, full of light. Artemis was a strong woman, already skilled at hunting.

The twins knew that the very first thing they must do was avenge the pain and suffering that Hera had inflicted on their mother. Protecting Leto would be a lifetime job for the twins. They traveled to the lands that had refused to admit Leto, and killed many of those

Apollo and Artemis Attacking Niobe and Her Children, painted in 1772 by Anicet-Charles-Gabriel Lemonnier. Speaking out against Leto was a huge mistake after her two children were born. They became experts at exacting vengeance. Niobe paid a heavy price for praising her children over Leto's.

who had turned her away. Later, they also killed the giant Tityus (TY-tee-us), son of Zeus. The giant attacked Leto, and she cried out for her children to help her. They shot him to death with their arrows. When Niobe (ny-OH-bee), daughter of Tantalus, insulted Leto by boasting that she had more children—and better ones—than Leto, Artemis and Apollo killed six of Niobe's sons and six of her daughters.

One day, Apollo wandered into the gorge of Parnassus. He did not realize it was Python's lair—the very Python that Hera had sent after Leto when she was looking for refuge. The snake was guarding a rock at the spot that one day would be known as Delphi. When Apollo saw the creature, he knew he had to destroy it with his silver bow and arrow. They had been specially made for him by Hephaestus, the god of fire.

Quietly, carefully, he snuck up on Python as it slumbered. He aimed. He fired. It was a direct hit! According to the *Homeric Hymn to Apollo,* "Then she, rent with bitter pangs, lay drawing great gasps for breath and rolling about that place. An awful noise swelled up unspeakable as she writhed continually this way and that amid the wood: and so she left her life, breathing it forth in blood." Then Apollo smiled with victory and boasted over the beast, saying, "Now rot here upon the soil that feeds man!"[4] The place where Python rotted under the sun became known as Pythos, and for killing the

Apollo slays Python. To commemorate the victory, Apollo founded the Pythian Games.

monster, Apollo became known as Pythian Apollo.

There was a price to be paid for this death. Gaia, Python's mother, was furious, and she asked Zeus to punish his son. Zeus banished Apollo from Mount Olympus and sentenced him to serve King Admetus (ad-MEE-tus) in Thessaly for nine years—as a cowherd!

King Admetus had no idea that a god was in charge of his cows. He only knew that he liked and trusted this man. Over the years, the two became good friends. Apollo was treated so well that he promised Admetus that one day, when death came for the king, he would arrange it so that another could take his place and he could live on. Years later, when death arrived for Admetus, Alcestis (al-SES-tis), his beloved wife, offered to take his place. At the last moment, Hercules stepped in and allowed both of them to live.

Another Punishment

Apollo's tendency to get into trouble with his father and others did not end there, of course. For example, when Zeus found out that Apollo was plotting against Hera, he again banished him from Mount Olympus. This time, Apollo and Poseidon were sent to King Laomedon (lay-OH-meh-dahn) to help the king build strong walls around the city of Troy. The two gods worked diligently, and finally they were done. Instead of being paid handsomely, as the king had assured them, Laomedon refused to pay them at all. It fit his reputation—he was known for being a traitor.

Although the two gods returned to Mount Olympus, they were angry about the betrayal. To get revenge on the king, Apollo sent a

Heracles Delivering Hesione by François Le Moyne. Hercules, whose Greek name was Heracles, staged a daring rescue of Hesione. Before leaving the scene, he took a moment to kill the sea monster—but his troubles were not over. Where was his payment?

plague to Laomedon's land. At the same time, Poseidon sent a sea monster. When the king sought help against these problems, the gods advised him to sacrifice his daughter Hesione (heh-SY-uh-nee) to the sea monster. He quickly chained her to a rock. Her death looked certain—until Hercules happened by. After the king promised to reward him with a team of horses, Hercules rescued Hesione and killed the sea monster. When he tried to collect his prize, however, once again the king went back on his word. It would be his last deceit. Hercules killed him and several of his sons.

Apollo had many fights still before him—and many women to chase. As one of the most respected gods on Mount Olympus, he had just gotten started.

Artemis, the Angry Twin

The twin sister of Apollo was known as the virgin goddess of the hunt and wild animals. When she was only three years old, Zeus told her she could have anything she asked for. After giving it some thought, she named four things: an archery set, the world's mountains in which to play, a city in which to live, and eternal virginity. Zeus granted her wishes.

Artemis was a loyal sister and daughter, but she was notorious for her anger. She did not forget when someone slighted her, and she usually made them pay for it dearly. For example, when King Admetus was married, he and his bride did not make a sacrifice in Artemis' name. The goddess filled their honeymoon bed with snakes. Later, when Oeneus (EE-nee-us), king of Calydon in Aetolia, and his people did not dedicate a fall harvest to her, she sent a huge, fierce boar to ravage the village. The king had to call in a number of heroes to help him slay the beast. When a young man named Actaeon accidentally saw Artemis bathing, she turned him into a stag, and his own hunting dogs killed him.

During the Trojan War, Agamemnon, leader of the Greeks, claimed he was a better hunter than Artemis. The goddess was not pleased. She waited until a fleet of Greek ships was on the way to battle and changed the winds, stranding the men on a distant shore. She did not help Agamemnon until he apologized and made a sacrifice for her. In some myths, that sacrifice was Iphigenia (ih-fih-jih-NY-uh), his daughter.

She was a loving sister, but sometimes Artemis and Apollo displayed typical sibling rivalry. In Book 21 of *The Iliad,* Apollo argues with Poseidon, but shamefully declines to fight the more powerful "god of the earthquake." Artemis teases him for backing down in the face of Poseidon's challenge, saying:

> "So, the deadly immortal Archer runs for
>   dear life!—
> turning over victory to Poseidon, total victory,
> giving him all the glory here without a fight.
> Why do you sport that bow, you spineless fool?—
> it's worthless as the wind!"[5]

Artemis

The remains of the Temple of Apollo at Delphi still attract visitors to the slopes of Mount Parnassus. The temple was largely destroyed by an earthquake in 373 BCE and was rebuilt in 330 BCE.

APOLLO

CHAPTER 3

Becoming an Oracle

Before serving Admetus, Apollo was known as the god of light, truth, and healing. As his nine years as a cowherd passed, he also became known as the god of agriculture and cattle. People prayed to him to make their fruit ripen, make their harvests rich, and keep their crops safe from pests. One of his many names was Apollo Smintheus, or "lord of mice," because he drove the rodents and locusts out of the fields.

Apollo had developed a reputation for always telling the truth. He also had the gift of prophecy—he could predict the future—so he wanted to find a place where he could establish a trusted oracle. When his time of service to Admetus was up, he remembered the perfect place: Pythos. He had killed Python there, and he knew the lair was abandoned. Off he went.

When he arrived at Pythos, he built an altar in the middle of a sacred grove, then looked around and realized something was still missing. He needed priests! He could not be an oracle if there was no one to hear his predictions and spread them across the land. Apollo looked out across the ocean and spotted a ship full of sailors. He had an idea.

Transforming Back and Forth

Turning himself into a dolphin, Apollo jumped into the ocean and swam through the salty waters until he reached the ship. He leaped up on the deck, startling the sailors. Suddenly, the ship's oars seemed to take on a life of their own, and the sailors could not control them. The ship swerved off course and headed straight for shore. The crew was terrified.

Once they ran aground, Apollo slid off the ship, disappeared into the forest, and then returned—this time as the god he was. He told the confused men that unfortunately they would no longer see their homes or wives but instead would be charged with guarding his temple. The job had its advantages, though, as it brought great honor, and they were allowed to share in any of the prizes and gifts others bestowed upon Apollo. He also asked the men to call him Delphinius, or Delphinian, since they had first spotted him in the sea in the shape of a dolphin.[1] Pythos would also be called Delphi. Then he transformed the men from simple sailors to royal guardians.

Word got around about Apollo and his predictions. People came to ask him questions and get a glimpse into their futures. As Edith Hamilton describes him in *Mythology:*

> O Phoebus, from your throne of truth,
> From your dwelling place at the heart of the world,
> You speak to men.
> By Zeus' decree no lie comes there,
> No shadow to darken the word of truth.
> Zeus sealed by an everlasting right
> Apollo's honor, that all may trust
> With unshaken faith when he speaks.[2]

Apollo remained at Delphi for most of the year, but as winter approached, he often left to go to the mysterious land of the Hyperboreans (hy-per-BOR-ee-uns), a group of people devoted to him. No one is sure where this place was, other than beyond the North Wind, somewhere near the edge of the world in a place where the sun never stops shining. He returned to Delphi each spring.

One time, Hercules came to see Apollo at Delphi to ask his advice. He had been struck down by a terrible unknown disease and was searching desperately for a cure. When the oracle did not have an answer for him, he tore the temple apart in anger, then he tried to

Apollo's tripod was made of gold and sat over a deep chasm in the rock below. The advice he would give from atop his sacred spot was often so vague that people could interpret it any way they wanted.

steal the sacred tripod on which Apollo sat. He figured he would use it to start his own oracle. The god and the hero fought over it. Soon Artemis appeared to help her brother, and Athena arrived to help Hercules. Finally Zeus had to step in to separate the brawlers. He struck a thunderbolt between them to stop the battle.

A Musical Challenge

As the god of music, Apollo played the lyre, a musical instrument similar to a harp but smaller. Like other gods, Apollo was vain. When Marsyas (MAR-see-us), a satyr, declared he was a better musician than Apollo, the god challenged him to a contest. The winner could do whatever he wanted to the loser.

Apollo and the Nine Muses, painted by Hendrick van Balen. The nine muses—Calliope, Clio, Erato, Euterpe, Melpomene, Polymnia, Terpsichore, Thalia, and Urania—inspired artists, musicians, and poets. They were the daughters of Zeus and Mnemosyne, the goddess of memory. Apollo was often seen as their leader, and the muses could often be found at the throne of their father, singing of his greatness and the deeds of heroes. The word *muse* is the base of the words *music* and *museum.*

In some versions of this myth, the one to boast of his musical abilities was not Marsyas but Pan. With either version, the story ends the same way. The judges for this contest were the nine muses, plus Midas, the king of Phrygia. The muses were young women who followed Apollo whenever they could. They were believed to be the inspiration for all poems, stories, and songs.

Apollo played his lyre as only a god could. Animals and nymphs, maidens, and other deities came from far and wide to listen. Then Marsyas picked up his pipes, similar to a flute, and played them. The instrument, which had been a gift from the goddess Athena, played lovely music.

Athena had invented the pipes and loved the sound they made, but when she played them, Aphrodite and Hera laughed at her. Wondering what was so funny, she looked in the water and saw her reflection. Her cheeks were puffed out. Her face was red. "The sound was pleasing; but in the water that reflected my face I saw my virgin cheeks puffed up. I value not the art so high; farewell my flute!" she exclaimed.[3] In a fury, she tossed the pipes into the woods, where the satyr later found them and taught himself how to play.

Apollo and Marsyas, painted by Perugino in 1495. A musical competition was considered the best way to determine who was the better player, Apollo (right) or the boastful Marsyas.

The two contestants each played gloriously, but then Apollo surprised everyone by turning his lyre upside down and playing another song. He challenged Marsyas to do the same, but of course, he could not. The muses quickly determined that Apollo was the winner of the contest. Only Midas spoke out against the young god, declaring that he did not win the contest fairly. Apollo was not pleased. He punished Midas in a rather unusual way: He gave him the ears of an ass. As Hamilton relates: "Apollo said that he was merely giving to ears so dull and dense the proper shape."[4]

Apollo, Marsyas, and the Judgment of Midas, engraved by Melchior Meier in 1582. Apollo punishes Marsyas and gives Midas the ears of an ass. Annoying Apollo always seemed to result in more trouble than anyone expected. After challenging Apollo to a musical contest, Marsyas paid with his life, while Midas' appearance was forever changed.

Because Apollo won the contest, he could choose what to do with the satyr. He decided to hang him from a tall pine tree and strip off his skin. It was not long before Apollo regretted his brutality and destroyed his lyre. The blood of the satyr and the tears of those who mourned him created the river Marsyas.

The Oracle at Delphi

According to some historians, the Oracle at Delphi was the most important priestess in all of Greece. Delphi was considered the center of the world by the ancient Greeks. Inside the shrine, a priestess, or oracle, heard predictions through a crack in the stones. She then interpreted these messages and shared them with those who needed answers. Believers came from all over to have their most burning questions answered by the oracle. The information they received ranged from a simple answer about when they should make a specific sacrifice to complex responses about whether it was time to go to war.

It also played an important role in mythology. The oracle told Oedipus (EH-dih-pus) that he would kill his father and marry his mother. She counseled Orestes (or-ES-teez), Agamemnon's son, to kill his mother, Clytemnestra, and her lover to avenge the murder of Agamemnon.

The inspiration for the oracle's predictions was said to come from the vapors, or fumes, rising from a crack in the ground. The oracle would inhale these vapors, which would give him or her knowledge of the future. He or she would interpret these messages and use them to answer people's questions.

Were there actually fumes of some kind coming out of the ground? A survey of the area in the 1980s dismissed the idea. There were no signs of gases escaping from a crack or chasm in the ground or surrounding rocks. In 1995, however, some scientists returned to the site where the shrine was supposed to have been. They found cracks in the ground known as fissures. Rising out of them were several types of gases, including ethylene, a gas that smells sweet and tends to make people hallucinate or imagine things if they breathe it. Was ethylene the reason the oracles could tell such remarkable stories of what was to come? The scientists think so.

"Ethylene inhalation is a serious contender for explaining the trance and behavior," says Diane Harris-Cline, a college professor in Washington, D.C. How accurate those visions were is still unclear.[5]

Fumes rise under the Oracle at Delphi

Ancient Greece covered a large area on the Mediterranean Sea and included many tiny
islands. Thessaly, on the western coast of the Aegean Sea, is where Apollo worked as a
shepherd. His oracle was at Delphi. Ilium, in Phrygia, was the ancient name for Troy,
where Apollo joined the other deities and heroes to fight the Trojan War.

APOLLO

CHAPTER 4
A God in Love

Despite his power and good looks, Apollo was not successful in love. His one-sided passion for Daphne is an example. As hard as he tried, he could not get her to love him, and she was willing to be turned into a laurel tree rather than be with him.

Her response was not unusual, however. In the Greek and Roman myths, love affairs between the gods and mortals were common, but these affairs often ended in pain and suffering for the mortal. Affairs with gods didn't always end well for nymphs, either.

When Daphne was transformed into a laurel, Apollo cried, "Since you cannot be my wife, you shall assuredly be my tree. I will wear you for my crown. With you I will decorate my harp and my quiver; and when the great Roman conquerors lead up the triumphal pomp to the Capitol, you shall be woven into wreaths for their brows. And, as eternal youth is mine, you also shall be always green, and your leaf know no decay."[1]

Although he couldn't win Daphne, Apollo had quite a few romances. He fathered more than a dozen children with more than nine different women and nymphs. According to legend, he had only one daughter, Parthenos; the rest of his children were sons. They included Tenes, who founded the island of Tenedos; the seer Iamos; and musicians Linus and Philammon. His children inherited his gifts of prophecy, music, and knowledge of medicine. Some of them, such as Aristaeus (ayr-ih-STY-us), became immortal.

While out hunting one day, Apollo spotted Cyrene (sy-REE-nee), a water nymph who was also a huntress. When the god saw this beautiful maiden wrestling a lion with her bare hands, he knew he had to have her. He carried her away in his golden chariot. Later,

she gave birth to his son Aristaeus. Their son learned medicine and the arts of beekeeping, shepherding, and cheesemaking, and he became the father of Actaeon. Gaia made Aristaeus immortal, but Actaeon, who boasted of his hunting skills, was killed through the trickery of Artemis.

Cyrene loved hunting and watching over her father's cattle. Her strength and confidence caught Apollo's eye.

Aristaeus, carved by François-Joseph Bosio in 1817. The son of Apollo and Cyrene, Aristaeus was a healer. However, following in his father's footsteps, he pursued an unwilling wood nymph named Eurydice. When she fled into the forest to get away from him, she was bitten by a snake and died.

A Prophet Ignored

Apollo also fell in love with Cassandra (kuh-SAN-druh), and the results were disastrous for her. In most versions of the myth, she consented to be with him if he would give her the gift of prophecy. Apollo agreed, but once she had the gift, she refused to allow him to touch her. In *Fabulae,* Hyginus writes: "When Apollo tried to embrace her, she did not permit him. So Apollo brought it about that she should not be believed, though she gave true prophecies."[2]

Although no one believed Cassandra, her predictions were true. She spoke of what would happen at Troy, that Paris would begin the war and that a dangerous horse would spell the end for the Trojans. No one listened to her, and eventually she was put in a place for the insane. Later, she was given to Agamemnon (aa-guh-MEM-non) as part of the victory. She gave birth to his twins, but when he took her home to his palace, Agamemnon's wife, Clytemnestra (kly-tem-NES-truh), killed her.

Cassandra, painted by Evelyn De Morgan in 1898. Cassandra's gift for prophecy quickly became a curse. Many of the Greeks who heard her story could relate to her, knowing what it felt like to be doubted when telling the truth. If the people had actually listened to her predictions, the course of Greek mythology might have turned out quite differently.

Spurned Again and Again . . .

When Apollo pursued Castalia, another nymph, she also refused him. She threw herself into a fountain at Delphi. Later tales say that

anyone who drank those waters or listened to the sound would be inspired to write poetry.

When Apollo went after the nymph Sinope (SIH-noh-pee), she agreed to be his but only if he would grant her one wish first. He happily gave in—he would provide anything she wanted if only she would surrender herself to him. Sinope then told him her wish: to remain a virgin for the rest of her life. That was the end of that relationship.

Tragedy Strikes Again

Another love affair gone wrong happened when Apollo fell in love with Coronis (kuh-ROH-nus), daughter of King Phlegyas (FLEE-jee-us). When she was pregnant with Apollo's child, she fell in love with the mortal man Ischys (IS-kus). A beautiful white crow flew off to tell Apollo of her unfaithfulness. He was furious! He asked Artemis to kill Coronis, then he cursed the crow, turning its feathers black.

Artemis did as her brother asked, but as Coronis' body was placed on the funeral pyre, Apollo removed his future child from her womb. It was a boy, whom he named Asclepius (uh-SKLEE-pee-us). Not sure what to do with the child, Apollo gave him to the centaur Cheiron (KY-rohn), who was known for raising young people. Cheiron taught the boy about herbs and potions, and Asclepius grew up to be a great and talented physician. In fact, he became so skilled that he was able to raise the dead. When Hades, god of the dead, found this out, he complained to Zeus. Not sure how to respond, the king of the gods killed Asclepius with one of his thunderbolts. Apollo was enraged but knew better than to attack his powerful father. Instead, he went after the Cyclopes, who had taught Zeus how to use thunderbolts in the first place.

Apollo's Other Loves

Apollo also fell in love with a number of boys and men. One of them was the Spartan prince Hyacinthus (hy-uh-SIN-thus). Like Apollo, he

was very athletic, and the two enjoyed playing sports together. One day, they were practicing how to throw a discus, a heavy metal disc that requires strong arms and skill to throw any distance. Although they did not realize it, they were being watched closely by Zephyrus (ZEH-fuh-rus), the god of the west wind. He also fancied Hyacinthus and was jealous of his relationship with Apollo. In anger, he shifted the wind just as Apollo tossed the discus. It went off course and hit Hyacinthus in the head, killing him instantly.

Apollo was frantic, but there was nothing he could do. To remember and honor the love he had for this young prince, he made a flower grow where the boy's blood had dripped upon the ground. "Thou diest, Hyacinth," said Apollo, "robbed of thy youth by me. Thine is the suffering, mine the crime. Would that I could die for thee! But since that may not be thou shalt live with me in memory

The Death of Hyacinthus, painted in 1752 by Giovanni Battista Tiepolo. Apollo's grief at the loss of Hyacinthus was overwhelming. By turning his lover into a flower, he kept his body from being claimed by Hades, god of the Underworld. Some myths say that by becoming a flower, Hyacinthus became immortal.

and in song. My lyre shall celebrate thee, my song shall tell thy fate, and thou shalt become a flower inscribed with my regrets."3 This flower is known as the hyacinth.

Another of Apollo's loves was Cyparissus (kuh-PAH-rih-sus), a distant relative of Hercules. As a gift, Apollo gave him a sacred deer. The young man tamed the deer and it became a favored pet. One hot summer day, when the deer was sleeping in the shelter of some trees, Cyparissus, thinking he was just any deer, threw his javelin and hit and killed the cherished animal. Absolutely heartbroken, the boy could not stop crying. He begged Apollo to kill him for what he had done. He wanted to cry for all eternity. Instead, the god turned him into a tree known as the cypress. According to one translation of the story, Apollo said, "All eternity I will weep for you, wonderful youth, and you in turn will partake of the sadness of others. Stand then from now until forever beside those stricken by sorrow."4 The cypress tree continues to be a symbol of grief.

Apollo was well known for his love life. He was also known for his role in the Trojan War. He would help end the war—and kill one of its greatest heroes.

Cyparissus grieves over the loss of his sacred pet deer.

Although the lyre is considered Apollo's musical instrument, he was not the first god to have one. His sacred stringed instrument was invented by Hermes, son of Zeus and Maia (MY-yah), a nymph.

Hermes was known as a trickster. On the day he was born, he tricked a tortoise into coming into his house, where he killed it and used its shell to make a lyre. He hid his new invention in his cradle and set off to find some meat. He found Apollo watching Admetus' cows and stole fifty of them. To cover his tracks, he made the cows walk backward so that their hoofprints would point toward the barn.

After traveling all night, Hermes settled near the river Alpheus and built a fire. He killed two cows and roasted them, then offered up eleven servings to the Olympians. Later, he went home and crawled into his cradle.

Apollo was already on Hermes' trail. He came to Maia's home and said, "Child, lying in the cradle, make haste and tell me of my cattle, or we two will soon fall out angrily. For I will take and cast you into dusty Tartarus and awful hopeless darkness, and neither your mother nor your father shall free you or bring you up again to the light, but you will wander under the earth and be the leader amongst little folk."[5]

Hermes denied stealing anything and ran to Olympus. When the two arrived in the hall of Zeus, Apollo accused Hermes of stealing, and Hermes pretended to be an innocent babe not capable of such a deed. Zeus told them to look for the cows together. Hermes led Apollo to them, then pulled out his lyre and began singing. Apollo was amazed. "Slayer of oxen, trickster, busy one, comrade of the feast, this song of yours is worth fifty cows and I believe that presently we shall settle our quarrel peacefully."[6] The two made a trade. Hermes gave Apollo the lyre, promising never to steal it back. Apollo gave Hermes a staff and the right to herd cattle and sheep.

Apollo and Hermes by Annibale Caricci

Chryses, a priest to Apollo, attempts to ransom his daughter, Chryseis, from Agamemnon (from about 350 BCE). When Agamemnon refused to give Chryses' daughter back to him, he called down the wrath of Apollo and changed the course of the Trojan War.

APOLLO

CHAPTER 5

A God at War

The Trojan War—the epic battle between the Greeks and the Trojans—began around 1200 BCE and lasted ten years. Many stories and myths from that time have been lost, but one of the main sources for the tale is Homer's *Iliad*. Through a series of twenty-four books, or chapters, the poet tells what happened over several weeks during the last year of the war. He details the courage of some and the brutality of others. He tells of brave battles and painful defeats. The epic paints a clear picture of the Greek myths and heroes, showing how the Greeks believed the gods affected the lives of mortals. Apollo plays a vital role in the story.

As the Greek soldiers camp by the shores of Troy, weary of waiting for the Trojans to give up Helen or engage in battle, they begin fighting among themselves. Agamemnon, their leader, dares to anger Apollo's priest Chryses (KRY-sees) by refusing to return his daughter, Chryseis (krih-SAY-iss), whom Agamemnon had won in battle. The old man begs Agamemnon:

> Just set my daughter free, my dear one . . . here,
> accept these gifts, this ransom. Honor the god
> who strikes from worlds away—the son of Zeus, Apollo![1]

Agamemnon refuses the priest, who cries to his protector for vengeance. Apollo descends upon their camp, raining arrows in the form of a plague on the Greeks for nine days:

> Down he strode from Olympus' peaks, storming at heart
> with his bow and hooded quiver slung across his shoulders.

The arrows clanged at his back as the god quaked with rage,
the god himself on the march and down he came like night.
Over against the ships he dropped to a knee, let fly a shaft
and a terrifying clash rang out from the great silver bow.
    . . . he cut them down in droves—
and the corpse-fires burned on, night and day, no end in sight.[2]

The seer Calchas (KAL-kus) tells the soldiers that Agamemnon must return Chryseis—and sacrifice 100 of their finest bulls—to soothe the god. Agamemnon argues, then finally agrees, but only if he can take Achilles' girl, Briseis (brih-SAY-iss).

When Chryseis is returned, Chryses again prays to Apollo: "Now, at last, drive his killing plague from the armies of Achaea!"[3] A sacrifice is made,

    And all day long
they appeased the god with song, raising a ringing hymn
to the distant archer god who drives away the plague,
those young Achaean warriors singing out his power,
and Apollo listened, his great heart warm with joy.[4]

Agamemnon has angered and insulted Achilles, who refuses to fight because he is so upset. The rest of the men begin to lose their inspiration on the battlefield as well—and once again, the Greeks are in trouble.

The Death of a Hero

During the Trojan War, Apollo fought on the side of the Trojans, while Athena helped the Greeks. At one point, as Achilles chases a group of Trojans, Apollo disguises himself as a soldier and leads the great warrior away from the other people, allowing them to escape. Once the others are safe, he reveals who he is to Achilles, who knows that killing a god is not possible. "You've blocked my way,

The Rage of Achilles, a 1757 painting by Giovanni Battista Tiepolo. To appease Apollo, Agamemnon gave Chryseis, his war prize, back to her father. When he asked for Briseis, the war prize of Achilles, to take her place, he angered his greatest warrior instead.

you distant, deadly Archer, deadliest god of all," Achilles angrily tells him. "Now you've robbed me of great glory . . . Oh I'd pay you back if I only had the power at my command!"[5]

Apollo also helps bring about the death of Patroclus, the dear friend of Achilles. Disguised as a man named Asius, Apollo confronts Hector, son of Priam (the king of Troy) and one of the fiercest Trojan soldiers. He goads Hector into facing Patroclus. Apollo then enters the battle himself, creating as much confusion as possible. In the meantime, in an attempt to rally the morale of Achilles' men,

Patroclus goes into battle wearing Achilles' armor, ready to battle Hector. He is winning, slaying many men quickly, when suddenly Apollo, who has come to Hector's rescue a number of times, reaches out and hits him on the head from behind, knocking off his helmet and stunning him.

> Yes, the lord Apollo met you there in the heart of battle,
> the god, the terror! Patroclus never saw him coming,
> moving across the deadly rout, shrouded in thick mist
> and on he came against him and looming up behind him now—
> slammed his broad shoulders and back with the god's flat hand
> and his eyes spun as Apollo knocked the helmet from his head
> and under his horses' hoofs it tumbled, clattering on . . .[6]

Along with losing his helmet, Patroclus also loses the armor protecting his heart:

> and lord Apollo the son of Zeus
> wrenched his breastplate off. Disaster seized him—
> his fine legs buckling—
> he stood there, senseless—[7]

As Patroclus struggles to stay on his feet and keep fighting, Hector moves in.

> Hector waiting, watching
> the greathearted Patroclus trying to stagger free,
> seeing him wounded there with the sharp bronze
> came rushing into him right across the lines
> and rammed his spearshaft home,
> stabbing deep in the bowels, and the brazen point
> went jutting straight out through Patroclus' back.
> Down he crashed—horror gripped the Achaean armies.[8]

The death of Patroclus brings the mighty Achilles back into battle, and in his rage he kills Hector. Later, Apollo helps guide the arrow that Paris, the prince of Troy and abductor of Helen, shoots at the warrior Achilles. The target is hit, and Achilles' long history of success in war comes to an end.

Patroclus' death brought sorrow and anger to many of Achilles' men. Apollo's role in the young man's defeat soon resulted in the death of Hector. Achilles did not know it, but Apollo's influence over his fate had already been determined.

Victories and Celebrations

The Trojan War was not the only military action in which Apollo had a hand. For example, he helped Theseus in his war against the Amazons, and he was present in the war between the centaurs and the Lapiths. For helping the Athenians in wartime, the Greeks honored him with the festival of Boedromia, held in midsummer. To thank him for their victory over the Minotaur, they also held the Pyanopsia on the seventh day of October. In Sparta, during their

nine-day festival for Apollo called Carneia, no soldiers could leave Sparta to go to war. Celebrations held in honor of Apollo did not stop there. On the sixth and seventh days of either May or June, the Thargelia was held in Athens, focusing on fruit and wheat crops, while the island of Delos held a celebration in his name every four or five years.

Athletic contests were often part of ancient Greek festivals, but some contests were festivals unto themselves. The Pythian Games were held in Delphi every four years to honor Apollo—in years between the Olympic Games. The Pythian Games included chariot races and other athletic events, as well as contests in music and poetry. To honor the god, wreaths of laurel would be worn or given as prizes to contest winners.

Honor Among the Gods

While he may have been ridiculed on occasion by his sister, Artemis, Apollo was respected by the other gods. When he walked into the hall at Mount Olympus, the other Olympians would frequently stand up to honor him. His mother, Leto, would take his bow and quiver and hang them on a golden nail. Zeus always welcomed his son and served him ambrosia in a cup. It was clear that Apollo's parents were proud of his many abilities and the way he lived.

Whether speaking as a prophet or working as a lowly cowherd, playing beautiful music or slaying a fierce creature, Apollo was charming. To the ancient Greeks who listened to the stories of his romances, adventures, and victories, Apollo was someone they could admire and worship from afar.

Apollo

Ambrosia—Food of the Gods

Ambrosia and nectar were the food and drink of the gods. No one is sure what was in them. Some believe ambrosia may have been fruit, cheese, olive oil, or barley. Others suspect that it had some connection to honey. Honey was a rare treat in ancient Greece, and people might have believed that only the gods and goddesses could enjoy it on a regular basis. Some myths state that each day, doves brought this ambrosia to Zeus. He, in turn, handed it out to the other deities, including Apollo, on Mount Olympus.

Not only was ambrosia the perfect food, it had magical powers in a number of the Greek myths. Aphrodite, goddess of love, used it like perfume before trying to seduce a man. Achilles was covered in it as a baby to make him immortal (his heel was his only weak spot). Thetis (THEE-tiss), the mother of Achilles, covered the corpse of their friend Patroclus with it before putting him on the funeral pyre.

Ambrosia was sometimes referred to as a liquid, but nectar was the drink of the gods. It was guaranteed to take care of all the immortals' hunger and thirst. It was even used to make Aphrodite even more beautiful than she already was.

Ambrosia was supposed to be given only to gods. Mortals were forbidden to consume it. In fact, when a son of Zeus named Tantalus (TAN-tuh-lus) stole some and gave it to humans, he was condemned to eternal punishment in the Underworld. He was forced to stand in a pool of water with fruit trees surrounding him. When he dipped down for a drink or reached for the food, it would move just out of his reach. From his name comes the word *tantalize*.

The word *ambrosia* is still used to mean any kind of delicious food. Modern recipes for ambrosia typically include fruits (such as oranges and coconut) and sugar. Nectar is the sweet liquid produced by flowers that is used for making honey.

Torment, by Bernard Picart, painted in 1731

Chapter 1. Inspiration and Explanations

1. Thomas Bulfinch, "Apollo and Daphne," from *Bulfinch's Mythology: The Age of Fable, or Stories of Gods and Heroes,* Chapter III, online at http://www.sacred-texts.com/cla/bulf/bulf02.htm

2. Ibid.

Chapter 2. A Rough Beginning

1. *Homeric Hymn to Apollo,* translated by Hugh G. Evelyn-White, lines 51–61; online at http://ancienthistory.about.com/od/apollomyth/a/HomericHymnAp1_2.htm

2. Ibid., lines 83–88.

3. Ibid., lines 115–122.

4. Ibid., lines 355–363.

5. Homer, *The Iliad,* translated by Robert Fagles (New York: Penguin Classics, 1990), Book 21, lines 527–543.

Chapter 3. Becoming an Oracle

1. *Homeric Hymn to Apollo,* translated by Hugh G. Evelyn-White, line 500; online at http://ancienthistory.about.com/od/apollomyth/a/HomericHymnAp1_2.htm

2. Edith Hamilton, *Mythology* (New York: New American Library, 1989), p. 30.

3. Ovid, "Athena," *Fasti,* 6.697, accessed at http://homepage.mac.com/cparada/GML/Marsyas.html

4. Hamilton, p. 293.

5. Roach, John. "Delphic Oracle's Lips May Have Been Loosened by Gas Vapors" *National Geographic News,* August, 14, 2001, accessed July 30, 2008 at http://news.nationalgeographic.com/news/2001/08/0814_delphioracle.html

Chapter 4. A God in Love

1. Thomas Bulfinch, "Apollo and Daphne," from *Bulfinch's Mythology: The Age of Fable, or Stories of Gods and Heroes,* Chapter III, online at http://www.sacred-texts.com/cla/bulf/bulf02.htm

2. Hyginus, *Fabulae* 93, accessed at http://www.theoi.com/Text/HyginusFabulae2.html#93

3. Thomas Bulfinch, "Apollo and Hyacinthus," from *Bulfinch's Mythology: The Age of Fable, or Stories of Gods and Heroes,* Chapter VIII, online at http://www.sacred-texts.com/cla/bulf/bulf07.htm

4. Ovid, *Metamorphoses,* 10. 106: "Apollo and Cyparissus," online at http://www.theoi.com/Text/OvidMetamorphoses10.html

5. *Homeric Hymn to Hermes,* translated by Hugh G. Evelyn-White, lines 254–259, online at http://ancienthistory.about.com/library/bl/bl_text_homerhymn_hermes.htm

6. Ibid., lines 436–437.

Chapter 5. A God at War

1. Homer, *The Iliad,* translated by Robert Fagles (New York: Penguin Classics, 1990), Book 1, lines 22–24.

2. Ibid., Book 1, lines 51–60.

3. Ibid., Book 1, lines 543–544.

4. Ibid., Book 1, lines 562–566.

5. Ibid., Book 22, lines 17–25.

6. Ibid., Book 16, lines 916–922.

7. Ibid., Book 16, lines 933–936.

8. Ibid, Book 16, lines 952–959.

FURTHER READING

For Young Adults

Barber, Antonia. *Apollo and Daphne.* London, England: Frances Lincoln Children's Books, 1998.

Boughn, Michael. *Into the World of the Dead: Astonishing Adventures in the Underworld.* Toronto, Ontario: Annick Press, 2006.

Catran, Ken. *Voyage with Jason.* Verona, New Jersey: Simply Read Books, 2006.

Church, Alfred J. *The Iliad for Boys and Girls.* Chapel Hill, N.C.: Yesterday's Classics, 2006.

Cobblestone Publishing. *If I Were a Kid in Ancient Greece . . .* Peterborough, New Hampshire: Cricket Books, 2007.

Fontes, Ron, and Justine Fontes. *The Trojan Horse: The Fall of Troy: A Greek Legend.* Minneapolis, Minnesota: Graphic Universe, 2006.

Works Consulted

Bulfinch, Thomas. *Bulfinch's Mythology*. New York: Random House, 1998. Also online at http://www.sacred-texts.com/cla/bulf/index.htm

Cotterell, Arthur. *Classical Mythology*. New York: Lorenz Books, 2000.

Forty, Jo, editor. *Classic Mythology*. Los Angeles: Thunder Bay Press, 1999.

Graves, Robert. *The Greek Myths*. New York: Penguin Books, 1955.

Hamilton, Edith. *Mythology*. New York: New American Library, 1989.

Homer. *The Iliad*. Translated by Robert Fagles. New York: Penguin Books, 1990.

Homeric Hymns. Translated by Hugh G. Evelyn-White. http://ancienthistory.about.com/od/apollomyth/a/HomericHymnAp1.htm

Hyginus. *Fabulae*. http://www.theoi.com/Text/HyginusFabulae1.html

Moncrieff, A.R. Hope. *A Treasury of Classical Mythology*. New York: Barnes & Noble Books, 1992.

Ovid. *Metamorphoses*. Translated by Brookes More. Boston: Cornhill Publishing Co., 1922. http://www.theoi.com/Text/OvidMetamorphoses1.html

Roach, John. "Delphic Oracle's Lips May Have Been Loosened by Gas Vapors." *National Geographic News,* August, 14, 2001, accessed July 30, 2008. http://news.nationalgeographic.com/news/2001/08/0814_delphioracle.html

On the Internet

Apollo for Kids
http://greece.mrdonn.org/greekgods/apollo.html

Apollo, Greek God of Light
http://www.men-myths-minds.com/greek-gods-apollo.html

Heroic Myths
http://www.mythweb.com/heroes/heroes.html

Living Myths: Greek Myths
http://www.livingmyths.com/Greek.htm

The Myth Man
http://mythman.com/

Pictures of Apollo in art and architecture
http://www.greek-gods-and-goddesses.com/greek-god-apollo.html

Theoi, Greek Mythology
http://www.theoi.com/

ambrosia (am-BROH-zjia)—Something delicious to taste or smell, often considered the food of the gods.

centaurs (SEN-tars)—Mythical creatures that were half human (top) and half horse (bottom).

discus (DIS-kus)—A disk that weighs over two pounds and is thrown for distance as a sport.

ethylene (EH-thuh-leen)—A colorless, flammable gas with a sweet smell and taste.

fissure (FIH-shur)—A natural division or opening; a split in the earth.

hallucinate (huh-LOO-sih-nayt)—To imagine something that is not actually happening.

javelin (JAV-lin)—A light spear.

laurel (LAW-rul)—A small European evergreen tree, also known as a bay.

muse (MYOOZ)—One of the group of goddesses who inspired music, poetry, and writing.

myths (MITHS)—Stories or beliefs of a culture that help explain their world.

nectar (NEK-tur)—Ambrosia in the liquid form; the drink of the gods.

nymph (NIMF)—One of the beautiful maidens who lived in the sea, woods, mountains, or other natural setting.

oracle (OR-uh-kul)—Someone who tells important information, often about the future.

papyrus (puh-PY-rus)—An ancient form of paper.

prophecy (PRAH-fuh-see)—A prediction of what will happen.

pyre (PYR)—A pile or heap of wood for burning a dead body.

quail (KWAIL)—A small bird.

satyr (SAY-tur)—A creature that is part human and part horse or goat, known for chasing women.

spoils of war—The things the victors take from the losers in war, including treasures, horses, and women.

virginity (vir-JIH-nih-tee)—Purity; being a virgin.

INDEX